Secret
Sketchbook

Secret Sketchbook

The Back Streets of Hamburg

Ronald Searle

Weidenfeld and Nicolson
5 Winsley Street London W1

Originally published in France under the
title *Filles de Hambourg* by Jean-Jacques Pauvert, Paris

SBN 297 00108 6

Printed in Great Britain
by Lowe & Brydone (Printers) Ltd., London

Erotik Bücher

Reeperbahn
incident

Colibri
Hamburg
gr. Freiheit
19 Aug 67

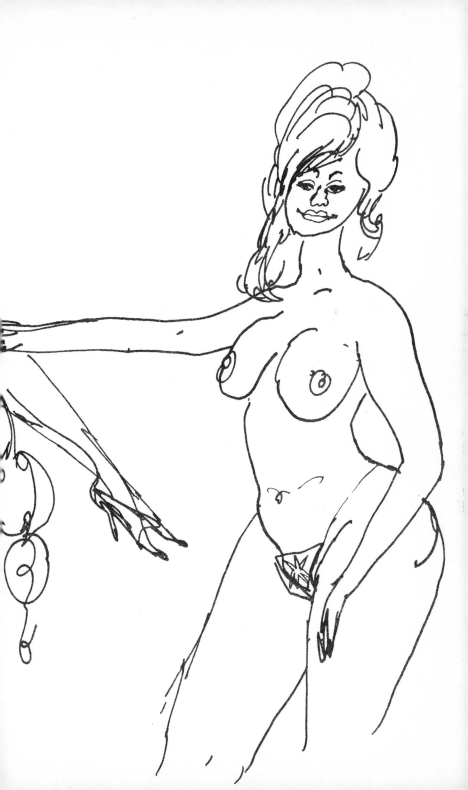

Caught in a
spiders web ...

Plastic poses

DURCHGANG FÜR JUGENDLICHE
VERBOTEN

DURCHGANG FÜR JUGENDLICHE
VERBOTEN

metal gate/barrier.

barrier each end of Herbertstraße

Herbertstraße

Safari
Cabaret.

Tabu
Cabaret

B-Girls

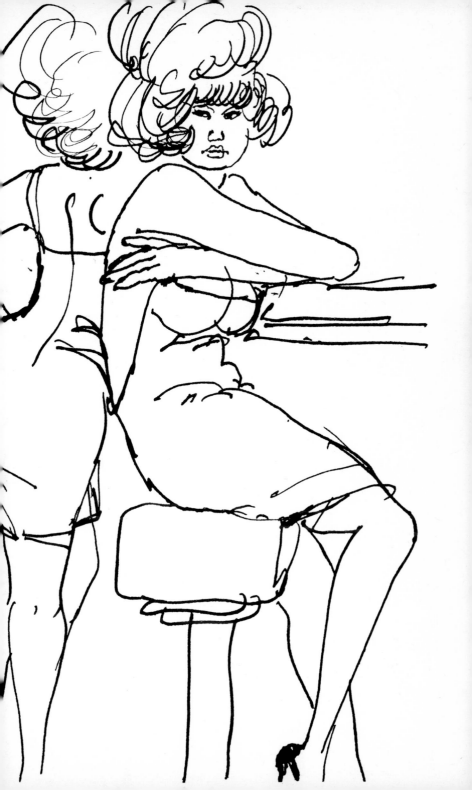

Hippodrom
Wrestling women

Schaug das'd
in Schwung
kimmst

Bierpreise
hell- export ½ ltr 2.00
hell Bock ½ ltr 2.50
Dunkel Bock ½ ltr 2.50
zuzügl. 10% f Bedienung

(on column)

ZILLERTAL
Bavarian Beer hall

s'chaug das'd in Schwung kimmst

11.35